Dear Judy & Jim –

Merry Christmas !!

Love,

Betsy & Kathy

2020

SCRUFFY
our loyal pandemic pooches
and the good, the bad, and the crazy haircuts we gave them

SHELLEY ROSS

ISBN: 978-0-578-74524-4

SCRUFFY BOOK PUBLISHING
New York, New York
www.scruffybook.com

SCRUFFY

our loyal pandemic pooches
and the good, the bad, and the crazy haircuts we gave them

SHELLEY ROSS

DEDICATION

——

For the tens of millions of people who have fought COVID-19 in the darkness.

For all the researchers, doctors, nurses, techs and carers, essential workers, frontline workers, teachers, and community volunteers… for all the neighbors, friends and family members, for anyone who has reached out to help ease someone's suffering during the Coronavirus Pandemic of 2020.

and

For the greatest pandemic partners ever imagined, my best friend and husband David and our loyal dog Scout.

ALL ABOUT THE FLOOF

The COVID-19 pandemic of 2020 will always be remembered for the unimaginable horror and fear as an invisible and deadly virus spread across the planet in just four months … and didn't stop. For so many of us *sheltering in place*, the only comfort came from our loyal dogs – ecstatic to spend 24/7 at home with us, instigating endless games of fetch and demanding regular belly rubs.

Suddenly rescue centers emptied out as word spread how the warm cuddle of a four-legged friend was a genuine and reliable elixir. Then soon enough, with groomers in lockdown, we were challenged to keep our joyful companions clean and mat-free on our own.

Up popped Instagram and YouTube DIY videos, scissors and razors ordered online. Many had to summon courage, some even spilled blood. A few did a truly outstanding job, but all seemed proud of their efforts nonetheless, as seen in the "floof" – the clippings not discarded but kept almost as a shrine to show our loyal dogs, and the whole world, how we tried our best.

FLOOF OF HESTON
Kent, United Kingdom

3

CHARLIE & LUNA
A MONOCHROMATIC MIX

Check out
our floof!

Don't we mix
well together?

Hair and photos by **AMY LANDRY** San Francisco Bay Area, California, USA
@charlie_hearts_luna

KIPPER & HOLLY
GENDER INEQUALITY?

The Pandemic Tale of Brother and Sister Cavapoos ...as told by Kipper.

Once upon a time in the faraway city of San Diego, CA, my sister Holly (she's the hot red-head) and I used to visit our beloved groomer every six weeks. It was heaven – we were shampooed, trimmed, manicured, massaged, and fluffed. No kidding, we walked out like movie stars.

THEN CAME THE PANDEMIC.

KIPPER & HOLLY

The story continues...

Look at us just nine weeks into the pandemic. The horror! I mean, Holly is still pretty cute, but I'm a hot matted mess. By May 17th, it was time for the scissors...in the trembling hands of Mom and Dad (mostly Dad).

Holly got away with a little butt trim, but...well... you'll see what happens to me.

Photos by **KAREN LEE** San Diego, California, USA | @kipperthecavapoo

Miss our groomer.

Love our hoomans.

Hair and photos by
KAREN LEE
San Diego, California, USA

@kipperthecavapoo

11

HENRY & CAILIN
IN FLUFFIER TIMES

We really didn't mind the shaggier version of ourselves.

Our pawrents thought otherwise.

If you think
Cailin looks
a little wacky,
wait until you
see me!

Hair and photos by
ANGELA & BILL NEYLON
Living the RV Life

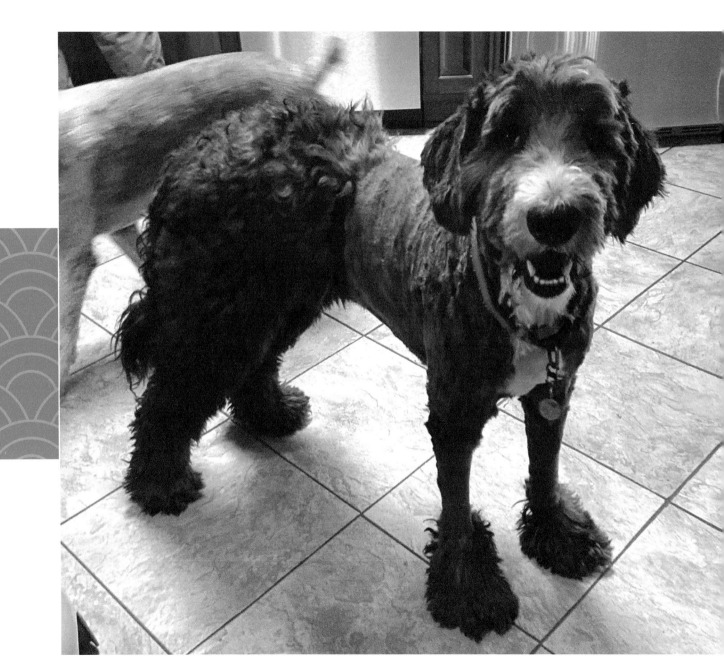

Oh, Henry!

I look like I am wearing work pants!

Seriously!

Who wears anything but yoga pants during a pandemic?!

Hair and photos by
ANGELA & BILL NEYLON
Living the RV Life

SUMMER

Hello there. My name is Summer and I'm a 3-year-old Shih Tzu.

You can almost feel the breeze blow through my lovely home-cut layers around my face and ears.

Thanks mom!

Hair and photos by **DENISE TUT** @denisetut

Jan 11

Media reports the first death in China from a virus that had infected dozens of people. The man who died was a regular customer at a market in Wuhan.

The United States confirms its first case in Seattle, WA – a man in his 30s who had traveled to Wuhan.

Jan 21

BY THE END OF
JANUARY 2020,
9,800 PEOPLE
WERE INFECTED

The World Health Organization
officially declares a global emergency
and the U.S. State Department warns
travelers to avoid China. The next
day, U.S. suspends entry into the
country by any foreign nationals who
had visited China in the past 14 days.
Immediate family of American citizens
are allowed to return.

Jan 30

213 PEOPLE
HAD DIED
WORLDWIDE

OATMEAL

For the first time ever,
my dad gave me a haircut.

It went about how you
would have expected.

DIXIE
THE COCKAPOO

These sad eyes belong to me, a dog named Dixie, as I sit in front of the floof.

I really miss my curls and if it weren't for #lockdown, I'd walk myself to Nana and Granddad's.

Hair and photos by @a_dog_named_dixie | Coventry, England

Loving my curls.

Missing my curls.

Hair and photos by
@a_dog_named_dixie
Coventry, England

25

PRESENTING...
SIR LAURENCE OLIVIER

I think I needed to be named after a less serious actor, don't you?

Hair and photos by
PEYTON
Bronxville, New York, USA

@olliepoodle2020

My pandemic cut
makes me look
like I'm about to
#burstoutlaughing.

BUFFY ZSA ZSA
BEFORE

Upside down happy dance of me, a rescue doggy in happy quarantine with Mom and my camera-shy rescue sister (not-seen-here, of course.)

Photo by **JENNIFER COHEN** Aspen, Colorado, USA

BUFFY
ZSA ZSA
AFTER

I feel like a star
celebrating my
2nd anniversary in
my forever home.

Hair and photo by **JENNIFER COHEN** Aspen, Colorado, USA

MANGO

Monday was Mommy's birthday,
so I woke her up like this!

She rubbed my belly and said I'm
adorable. Then mentioned,
"You're up for a haircut next week."

Ay, caramba!

Photo by @mango.shih tzu | Montevideo, Uruguay

MANGO

Our country, Uruguay, has had excellent COVID-19 intervention. Half of our cases were traced to one socialite who had flown in from Spain to attend a wedding with 500 guests on March 7th. Forty-four hoomans were infected that day. I'm so proud of our tracing.

Hair and photo by @mango.shih tzu | Montevideo, Uruguay

AUGGIE MAE
IN EVERYONE'S FAVORITE CHAIR

Hello there. I'm Auggie Mae the Sheepadoodle.

Isn't this chair the best? It fits me sooooo perfectly.

Photo by **SARAH NIEMANN** Denver, Colorado, USA | @auggie_the_sheepadoodle

AUGGIE MAE
AFTER

I put this picture here
so you can see –
"Hello it's me…"

Hair and photos by **SARAH NIEMANN** Denver, Colorado, USA | @auggie_the_sheepadoodle

NELLIE
EXERCISES PATIENCE

Original drawing of *Nellie the Cavapoo After* by Oscar Parry, *age 8.*

Hair and photo by © **NICOLA PARRY** Essex, United Kingdom | @parryphoto | @tinywolfnellie

Feb 11

The W.H.O. officially names the disease COVID-19 – an acronym for Coronavirus Disease 2019.

Italy becomes the first country in Europe to see the virus suddenly surge – from 5 cases to 150. This prompts officials to lockdown 10 towns southeast of Milan. Cases in 14 other countries will be traced to Italy.

Feb 23

Feb 29

Authorities announce that a patient near Seattle has died from the virus – thought to be the first COVID-19 in the U.S. Doctors will later discover two people died earlier.

MARCH 13, 2020
PRESIDENT
DONALD TRUMP
DECLARES
A NATIONAL
EMERGENCY IN
AMERICA

HOOTIE
THE GOLDEN DOODLE

#LooksLikeaCrimeScene

#NailTrimGoneWrong

#BloodSpatterEverywhere

#HurtThemMoreThanMe

Hair and photo by **VICKI LATOPOLSKI** San Luis Obispo, California, USA

DALHYA

Am I hiding or
just blending into
the counter top?

Hair and photos by
VANESSA ROULEAU & ADAM TINGSKOU Ottawa, Canada | @lefhoop

DALHYA

Neither.

Just hanging around with my new mini-me.

I think I love her.

Hair and photos by
VANESSA ROULEAU & ADAM TINGSKOU Ottawa, Canada | @lefhoop

L-O-L-A

No filter or mascara was used in the photographing of my eyelashes.

#shichonlashes

ZOLA

Dear Mom, don't you think a muzzle is a bit excessive for a haircut on a little Cairn Terrier like me?

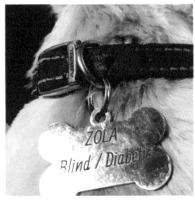

New cut, new tag.

I'm over it.

Hair and photos by **EMILY COLLINS** London, United Kingdom

DELAINO

It will be at least a week until I come out after this haircut.

Hair and photo by
COLETTE REISON
San Diego, California, USA

Or maybe I'll be okay by dinner.

LITTLE
MR. SUNSHINE

I'm a chocolate long-haired
Chihuahua named Mr. Sunshine.

Ya think Mom needs to leave my
grooming to the pros?!

Hair and photo by **KENDRA MUNGER** Toronto, Canada | @little_mr._sunshine

CASH & RAWLEY

Are these giant floof paws or the floof of Sasquatch?

Hair and photos by **LARRAINE ROSNER** Encino, California, USA

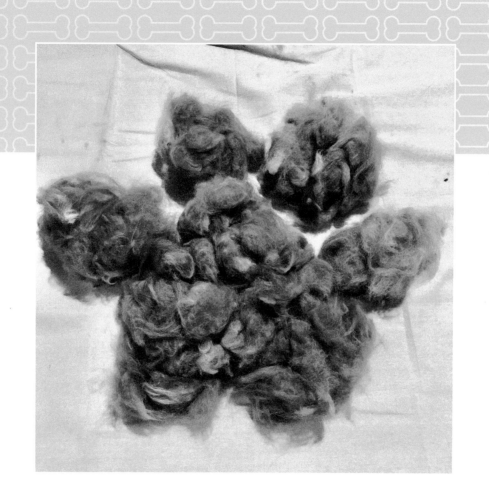

CASH & RAWLEY

Hi, we're Cash and Rawley – Tibetan Mastiff brothers rescued by our brave and beautiful forever Mom when we were 6 years old.

Our first hooman Mom passed away and we wound up in a shelter. We had a lovely home in San Fransisco where Mom was a dentist (and always took extra care of our teeth.) She was very young when she died. Everyone was sad; especially us..

It's not easy being orphaned when you weigh150 pounds. Would anyone ever take us both? Turns out, our new Mom-to-be said it was love at first sight. She brought us into our new home and helped us heal. Now we know, you can fall in love again.

Hair and photos by **LARRAINE ROSNER** Encino, California, USA

CASH & RAWLEY

We love to eat a lot, play a lot and take walks all around our new neighborhood.

Then came the pandemic.

We sheltered in with Mom and learned to make sure the "coast is clear," that no one else is around when we take our walks.

Hair and photos by **LARRAINE ROSNER** Encino, California, USA

Our grooming isn't something that can be delayed. We blow out our undercoat twice a year, pandemic or no pandemic.

It's especially crazy for me, Cash, I have the thicker undercoat which is harder because it's all brushed out by hand. Mom says the hours of brushing has made her arms really buff.

Our good friend's Mom filled six trash bags with his floof. There must be way to recycle it. Anyone see a market for Tibetan Mastiff floof scarves?

WHY IS EVERYONE TALKING ABOUT THE #QUARANTEENFIFTEEN?

EDDY

Eddy denies eating
Doggie Bonbons.

Photo by
RENÉE ANDERSON   Mason City, Iowa, USA | @eddychasingbear | #shichonpuppy

EDDY

It's not true that we don't have a sense of time.

Trust me when I say this is taking for-evah.

I may need a moment to gather my thoughts.

Hair and photos by
RENÉE ANDERSON   Mason City, Iowa, USA | @eddychasingbear | #shichonpuppy

EDDY

Can you believe all that
came off of me?!

Hair and photos by
RENÉE ANDERSON
Mason City, Iowa, USA

@eddychasingbear | #shichonpuppy

EDDY

I bet you're sorry
you fat shamed me.

Hair and photos by
RENÉE ANDERSON   Mason City, Iowa, USA | @eddychasingbear | #shichonpuppy

Happily
Eddy
After

I'm ready
for my
Zoom
calls now.

PENNY
GETS HER GIRLISH FIGURE BACK

How did a sweet little girl like me get trapped inside the body of a linebacker?

I'm turning into a St. Bernard right before my very own eyes.

Whew, I feel so much better... half my size... small enough to be offered a gazillion treats for my birthday.

Oh, happy me.

Hair, photos, and birthday party by
STEVEN & JULIE NELSON & FAMILY Salt Lake City, Utah, USA

TIKAL BEFORE

I'm sorry to say, you won't see this fluffy face for a while.

Photos by **SHAWN GOLDBERG** Toronto, Canada

TIKAL
AFTER

No words.

No woofs.

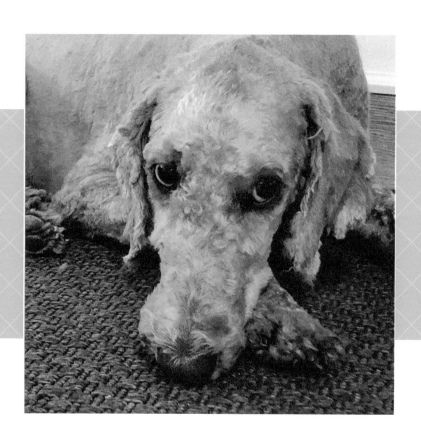

Sigh.

#itwillgrowback
#itwillgrowback
#itwillgrowback

PATRONUS
STRIKES A POSE

No iPhone photos for this service dog. On special occasions – like this grooming – my Mom takes out the big camera I can't pronounce and I sit here until she gets my best side… all of them.

SISI
THE WESTIE

Nothing like "tubby snacks"
while getting a trim!

Hair and photo by
ASHLEY HOLLY   Orange County, California, USA | @sisi_the_westie

BOGEY
#QUARANTINED4EASTER

It was Easter, and I had a funny feeling
Mom was up to no good.

           I was right;
           it was time to say goodbye to my floof.

Photo by
RACHEL JARDINIANO
Virginia Beach, Virginia, USA
@bogey_the_dood

83

BOGEY
THE DOOD
X2

I got a cut,
then a bath,
then another cut.

The woman was
obsessed!

She made me lay down and pretend I was asleep for this photo.

Hair and photos by
RACHEL JARDINIANO
Virginia Beach, Virginia, USA

@bogey_the_dood

85

Mar 16

President Donald Trump advises citizens
to avoid groups of more than ten. New York
City's public school system, the largest
in the nation with 1.1 million students,
announces it will close.

Several countries across Latin America announce
quarantines. Columbia and Costa Rica close borders.
France announces a lockdown.

Mar 17

Mar 23

Great Britain announces a
lockdown. The next day India
announces a 3-week lockdown
of its 1.3 billion citizens.

BY THE END
OF MARCH,
THE UNITED
STATES LEADS
THE WORLD IN
THE NUMBER
OF CONFIRMED
INFECTIONS:
81,321

BELLE

I swear I have eyes
in here somewhere.

Photo by
PAULINE McHUGH   Houston, Texas, USA | @belle_the_aldoodle

BELLE

I feel like a movie star without this pile of floof attached to me.

I'm ready
for my
close up!

Hair and photos by
PAULINE McHUGH   Houston, Texas, USA | @belle_the_aldoodle

TED

If you can't tell,
I'm a Welsh Terrier.

Really – just look
at my floof!

Hair and photos by **SHARON SALT** Staffordshire, Moorlands | @woolypaws

BODHI
THE
CAVOODLE

High-5 Mom for my first DIY haircut!

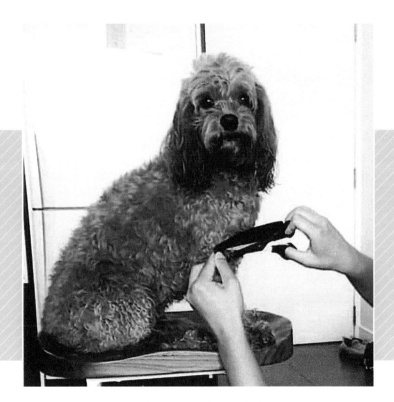

You rocked it!

LUNA

Can you guess my breed
(mix) from my floof?

Hair and photos by **E. HUMPHRIS** Cardiff, United Kingdom

LUNA

I am Luna the Yorchon: Bichon plus Yorkie.

Dad does the clipping while Mom feeds me treats to keep me still....

...like I would move with that electric whipsaw that close to me.

Hair and photos by **E. HUMPHRIS** Cardiff, United Kingdom

FLYNN
THE BICHON

Dad, wait, wait, wait ...

It's just a little mud!

FLYNN
THE BICHON

OH, YOU DID NOT.

Do you see how big you
made my nose look?!

Hair and photo by **KENNY FALCONER** Stonehaven, Scotland

GUINNESS
THE GIANT
(SCHNAUZER)

I'm a sweet girl
from Michigan.

I feel like I'm down a schnauzer.

TIPPY

So what if my mom cuts my hair.

We're in the midst of a pandemic. Don't judge.

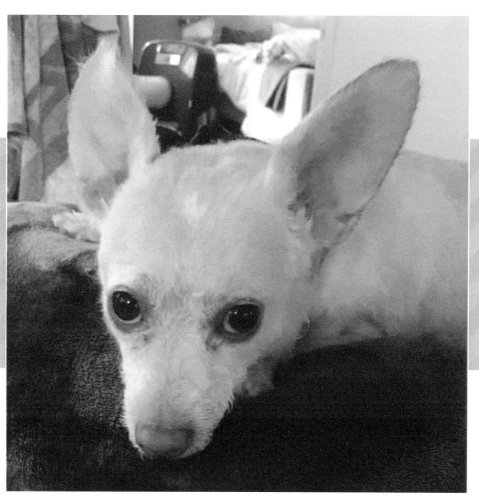

Hair and photos by **TAMMY McCULLAR**

QUARANTINE DOGGIE HAIRCUTS GONE VIRAL

EVIE

Evie's Story

April 22, 2020 was an average pandemic day at our home in Gloucester, U.K. when Mom decided to take an electric razor to Dad's beard. That little toddler fellow was frightened by the noise so Mom assured him it was safe that even I (an awesome English Labrador Retriever) wasn't afraid. She meant to just put the razor near me, but I got spooked and jumped. And well... this happened.

I may look like a piggy bank, but I became the star of one of the most "shared" dog photos of the 2020 COVID-19 pandemic.

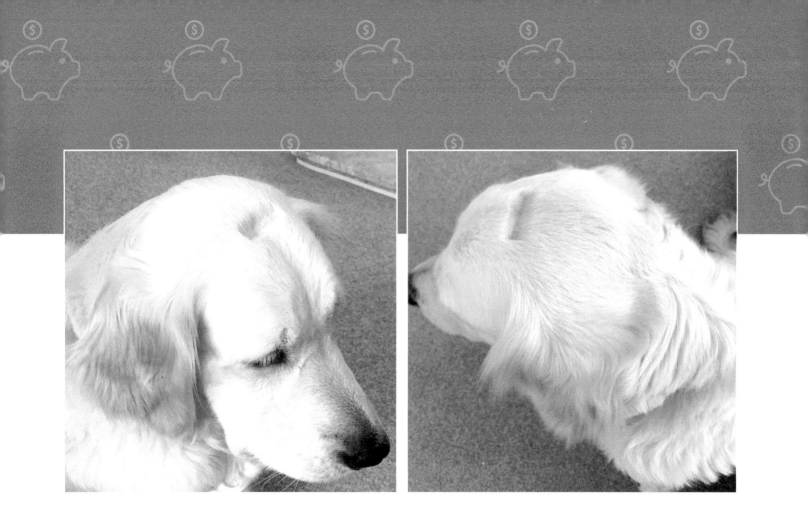

Hair and photos by THE SHARPE FAMILY Gloucester, United Kingdom

EVIE

Do I seriously look like a
piggy bank to you?

©Kennedy News and Media UK

Hair and photos by **THE SHARPE FAMILY** Gloucester, United Kingdom

MASH
THE MOST VIRAL POMERANIAN (EVER)

And you thought *YOU* were having a bad hair day?

Hair and photos by
HERMIONE OLIVIA
Sydney, Australia

@bossmash

HOPPER
THE ENGLISH GOLDENDOODLE

Wut?

Is this not the mug of a dog who is plotting his revenge for this home haircut?

Hair and photos by **KATIE McCURRY** Abbeville, South Carolina, USA | @hopperpupper

SLEEK
CELESTE

I think my hoomans were
tailors in another life.

Hair and photo by **ODIE CAWLEY** San Luis Obispo, California, USA | www.odiesdoodles.com

CROSBY

I'll be studying Morse code
before my next haircut.

I can't talk, but I can tap.

[MAYDAY! THIS IS CROSBY THE COCKER.
MY GROOMER IS IN SOME PLACE CALLED
"LOCK DOWN" AND MOM IS COMING AT
ME WITH SCISSORS.]

Hair and photo by
JENNIFER FAUST   Wentzville, Missouri, USA | @crosbythecocker

Apr 2

Global infections top 1 million people in 171 countries across 6 continents. The pandemic has put 6.6 million Americans out of work.

Apr 17

President Donald Trump encourages rightwing protests against social distancing and other restrictions in certain states.

British Prime Minister Boris Johnson, who has had the virus for 10 days, is moved into intensive care.

Apr 6

IN THE MONTH OF
APRIL, THE NUMBER
OF PEOPLE
INFECTED WITH
THE VIRUS TRIPLES
TO OVER 3 MILLION
AROUND THE
WORLD

President Trump suggests injecting
bleach or isopropyl alcohol could
help fight COVID-19. The makers
of Clorox and Lysol implore
Americans not to.

Apr 23

217,769
DEATHS ARE
RECORDED

FRIZZY CHEWBARKA
& HIS SISTER RUSSEL

Their story, as told by Frizzy

It's May 2, 2020. Happy International Doodle Day.
I celebrate because my sister is definitely a doodle mix. She came here as a puppy so I know her dad was a Chihuahua and her mom was a #chihuahuapoodle. My lineage is a little less certain. My first hooman got me as a puppy and when I was four, listed me as a #chihuahuapoodlemix "free to a good home." It turned out to be the greatest home, even though my forever Mom calls me "a rude narcissist." I'm not, really, I'm just a natural showman.

Photo by FRIZZY'S MOM London, Ontario, CA

FRIZZY CHEWBARKA

The minute I started playing with Russel's floof, I knew I was up next for the dreaded #quarantinecut.

I'm still frizzy
on the inside.

Hair and photos by
FRIZZY'S MOM
London, Ontario, CA

CALEB & CHLOE

Hi, Caleb here.

If you think I'm fancy,
wait until you see my
sister, Chloe!

Hair and photos by
JIN KIM

@thefashiondesigner

CALEB & CHLOE

I'm even adorable before my haircut!

I'm nearly as cute
as my brother.

Turn back a page if
you don't remember
just how darling he is.

Hair and photos by
JIN KIM

@thefashiondesigner

BATH TIME FOR FUR BABIES

MAIZEE SCHMIDT

This is my big sister Sarah's idea of a dry shampoo.

I think she gets her sense of humor from our Dad.

Photo by **LEXIE JOHNSON** Provo, Utah, USA

ESTELLE-LOUISE

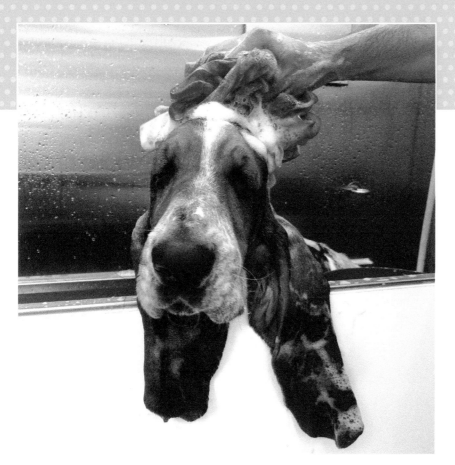

My ears are way too big for this bathtub, but who's complaining? I'm just here for the head massage.

HUGO

#mini-doodle

#lovestastinghisbathwater

Photos by
ASTA HARDLASDOTTIR
Braintree, Massachusetts, USA

@happydoghugo

LITTLE PABLO ESCOBARK

Sorry my American friends, I'm hiding out in Hong Kong. But even I cannot escape the doggo bath torture.

I do believe friends make everything better.

Photo by @littlepabloescobark | The Murray Hotel, Hong Kong

May 21

Global COVID-19 cases pass 5 million. It had been at 4 million less than two weeks prior. It soon grows to more than 100,000 cases every day.

MEMORIAL DAY –
All states are in various
stages of reopening,
including bars and beaches.

May 25

US CASES TOP
4.3 MILLION

33 COUNTRIES
BAN AMERICAN
TRAVELERS

KENJI & SPENCER – THE PEEKAPOO BROTHERS

Welcome to a day in our home spa!

Dad says he has to take a gazillion photos just to get one with our heads like this.

Photos by @kenjispencer | Sydney, Australia

KENJI

Oh,
brother!

SPENCER

Photos by
@kenjispencer

Sydney, Australia

The art of the trim with Spencer.

Hair and photos by @kenjispencer | Sydney, Australia

Good night!

Quarantining
is exhausting.

FRIZZY CHEWBARKA

Hi, it's me again, this time in the bath.

#bathdaybetrayal

Photos by
FRIZZY'S MOM
London, Ontario, CA

KABOOM, SKYE FANCY & BREEZE

Our multi-fibre luxury robes were designed by our two Dads because we all just hate the hair dryer.

Photo by
DA'QUAN O'NEAL & EUGENE BLAGMOND
Philadelphia, Pennsylvania, USA

@fancykaboompawtique | @breezingintheskye

EDIE SEDGWICK

If no one can find me, then I don't have to take a bath.

Photos by her companions
MAUREEN & STEVIE VAN ZANDT
Greenwich Village, New York, USA

EDIE SEDGWICK

Voila!

Photos by her companions **MAUREEN & STEVIE VAN ZANDT**
Greenwich Village, New York, USA

KOVA THE ZU

It became clear on one of my increasingly rare car rides, I could no longer see through my hair.

It was a quality of life issue.

Out came the new pandemic emergency grooming kit. Whatever Mom lacked in experience, she made up for in restraint. (Obviously I'm kidding. Just look across the page.)

AAAAAAGH!

Who knew I had freckles?

Hair and photos by
KIM VISCARRA
Lanham, Maryland, USA

@Kova_The_Zu

PIPER'S
PANDEMIC AUDITIONS

My story is pretty simple. Mom used to be an actress. So when we were quarantined together, she liked to dress me up for various movie roles.

As a Cavalier King Charles Spaniel, I was at least spared the #lockdownhaircut.

Costume design and photos by CARLEEN SIMONE New York, New York, USA

PIPER

Then, around week six, I started hearing Mom complain that with all the baking and cooking and hyper-cleaning, she felt like a 1950's house wife. I kept thinking, "what's that?"

And, as always, as if Mom can read my mind, she just showed me.

I totally get it now.

Costume design and photos by CARLEEN SIMONE New York, New York, USA

FRIZZY

And this is what happens
when *my* Mom gets bored.

#lockdownrainbowhair

Hair and photo by **FRIZZY'S MOM** London, Ontario, CA

A CAUTIONARY TAIL:
LILLI

AUTHOR'S NOTE:
this was the photo that launched "Scruffy."

An old friend had posted this photo of Lilli's crooked little tail that looked like it had been run over by a lawnmower.

It was April, 2020 and I knew this must be happening all over the world.

It was.

Hair and photos by **LISA R. "MOM" COHEN** New York, New York, USA

ASH
THE GOOD BOY ON THE COVER

You would never guess by the photo on the cover that I have this much energy.

Hair and photos by **LARAINE LOH** London, United Kingdom | @ashthemaltipoo

SCOUT
THE POLISH LOWLAND SHEEPDOG

Full disclosure: I am the fur baby of the author of this book.

My mom and I would like to thank all the dogs and their families who offered their great photos in support of our scientists fighting COVID-19. Woof.

Hair and photos by **SHELLEY ROSS** *President, The Cure Alliance*

Jun 12

With 70,000 new cases reported from the past week, Florida shatters the national record as plans to re-open schools move forward. Thirty-one states show increases. National death rate climbs after previous declines.

On this day more new cases are reported globally in a single day than ever before: 166,099. In America an alarming surge in the sunbelt states.

Jul 17

THE SUMMER SURGE OF 2020

Jul 28

In nine weeks, the number of global COVID-19 cases tripled to over 16.5 million.

As we end the first pandemic summer, the Coronavirus is still on the march with no sign of weakening. Global cases are soaring over 23 million, deaths nearing one million. Chaos remains a hallmark of the pandemic in America, with the continued politicization of science and medicine.

Dr. Antony Fauci, the top scientist in the U.S. for infectious disease and the pandemic, reports in early August that he and his family had received death threats. Certainly, the COVID-19 crisis in America: the #1 issue for the presidential election.

Beyond the bleak picture of the moment, there is hope. Early phases of vaccine trials are showing promising results. Early intervention with blood thinners, plasma, and more has saved lives. Hopefully, with immediate UC-MSC treatment for lungs, the number of patients who languish on ventilators will be greatly diminished, even avoided.

This pandemic is the greatest global challenge of the 21st Century. So much is still up to us, to wear masks, even face shields. Avoid crowds – especially indoors.

Keep a social distance of six feet. And wash your hands regularly for at least two choruses of Happy Birthday.

Stick to these rules as if your life depends on it, because it just may.

A LETTER
FROM THE PRESIDENT
OF THE CURE ALLIANCE

THE CURE ALLIANCE

I hope you enjoy reading "Scruffy," as much as I did curating it. Please note that **100% of the profits** from the purchase of this book goes directly to ongoing scientific research to end human suffering caused by COVID-19. You might have read about or heard the recent news of the results of our FDA-authorized clinical trial. Due to the efforts of The Cure Alliance, we now have a powerful new weapon, UC-MSCs (umbilical cord-derived mesenchymal stem cells), to fight the lung damage seen in the most severe cases of the virus.

The Cure Alliance has come a long way from its launch ten years ago. Back then our founder, Dr. Camillo Ricordi, imagined a virtual place for elite scientists from around the world to share knowledge and tear down barriers to curing all diseases, helping to move their successes in the lab to the patient's bedside. From his perch as Director of the Diabetes Research Institute and Cell Transplant Center at the University of Miami's Miller School of Medicine, he knew we no longer cured diseases in the 21st century and the process of advancing a new drug or treatment took too many years and billions of dollars.

The Cure Alliance went to work in Washington, D.C., into the chambers of subcommittee working on The 21st Century Cures Act; we co-sponsored multiple World Stem Cell Summits encouraging thousands of scientists to collaborate and advance the uncharted waters explored by the Regenerative Medicine Foundation. Each year there was a flood of exciting new presentations heralding a new era of discovery: unleashing the power of human stem cells. We could now easily distinguish the stem cell research superstars from the opportunists opening up the bogus clinic down the street. Unfortunately, where there is discovery, there are always con artists.

Meanwhile, The Cure Alliance, now an official 501 (c) (3) non-profit organization, waded deeply into FDA territory successfully pressing the government not to over-regulate stem cell research or create new red tape which could have crippled the advancement of important treatments, including the one our Cure Alliance scientists were about to advance. Right at the start of the Coronavirus pandemic, Dr. Camillo Ricordi called upon our membership and leadership to pivot our mission from curing all diseases to ending the suffering caused by just one: COVID-19. He called for a "mini-Manhattan Project" with fellow scientists specializing in pulmonary medicine, critical care, and more. In no time, the group drafted a 150-page proposal to present to the FDA to test UC-MSCs to repair the lung damage seen in the most severe COVID-19 cases. Dr. Ricordi already had FDA authorization to see if UC-MSCs could reduce inflammation that impairs the pancreas at the onset of diabetes. For three years of research had navigated a challenge: the UC-MSCs stubbornly migrated directly to the lung instead of the pancreas.

For Dr. Ricordi, COVID-19 presented an opportunity to see if the treatment would work best on what seemed like its own chosen target, the lungs. At the same time, a scientist in China reported success with UC-MSCs on a few random patients. In pockets around the world, a few doctors here, a handful there were reporting more success. But did the patients try any other treatment as well? How was the lung damage and repair documented? Was there anything in the patient's history that might explain reversal? Any unreported failures? A strict scientific investigation was needed. In less than a week, on April 9, 2020, the FDA authorized Dr. Camillo Ricordi and his team to conduct a randomized clinical trial to scientifically prove whether or not UC-MSCs could repair the lung damage caused by COVID-19. The clinical trial was fully donor-funded with money raised by The Cure Alliance plus generous donations from The North America Building Trades Union (NABTU), the Diabetes Research Institute Foundation (DRIF) and the Barilla Group and family. You can read the stunning clinical trial results posted on our website www.thecurealliance.org.

Our work now begins to assure this simple IV infusion of UC-MSCs will be widely available to all, and free or at minimum cost. One umbilical cord can create 10,000 doses, but it still must be scaled, manufactured, and distributed. Again, 100% of profits from "SCRUFFY" will go directly to this effort, and more science research to end suffering caused by COVID-19.

Please buy a book for a friend or two. Honor a loved one, a carer, a front-line or essential worker with a book. Ask your corporation to buy in bulk as company gifts. Donate to us directly online at **www.thecurealliance.org/donate.** Help us beat COVID-19 and return to the daunting task of working on cures for the other chronic, debilitating and fatal diseases you or someone you love are fighting.

Thank you,
Shelley Ross, *President of The Cure Alliance*

MY COVID-19 JOURNAL

This book was purchased by _____

I gift this book to _____

○ myself   ○ my quarantine partner   ○ my friend   ○ our family   ○ the one I miss the most

I hope to honor _____

○ loved one(s)   ○ doctors   ○ nurses   ○ frontline workers

○ essential workers   ○ scientists   ○ those who have fought COVID-19

Today's date _____

Today's global COVID-19 cases _____

For up-to-date numbers, go to coronavirus.jhu.edu.

I first heard about the pandemic when...

_____

_____

_____

At first, I thought...

_____

_____

_____

When the discussion turned to _locking down_ and _sheltering in_, I went out and bought...

_____   _____   _____

_____   _____   _____

There was a mass shortage of...

_____   _____   _____

_____   _____   _____

During the pandemic…

○ I stayed at home   ○ I worked from home   ○ I was an essential worker

I knew _____ people who were infected with the virus.

The pandemic changed how I feel about…

_____

_____

_____

The toughest moment for me was…

_____

_____

_____

I watched the news _____ hours a day on _____

My favorite pandemic TV shows to binge were...

_____   _____   _____

_____   _____   _____

_____   _____   _____

I read...

_____   _____   _____

_____   _____   _____

_____   _____   _____

I wore masks made of...

_____

What I missed the most was...

_____

_____

If I had to name *one* positive aspect of the pandemic, it would be...

_____

_____

_____

People who know me well, would be surprised that I...

_____

_____

_____

I want the next generations to know...

_____

_____

_____

A safe and effective COVID-19 vaccine was announced on _____

RANDOM THOUGHTS

ACKNOWLEDGMENTS

SCRUFFY, as you may already know, is a Cure Alliance fundraising initiative to advance the success of our recent FDA-authorized clinical trial which used a simple IV infusion of UC-MSCs (umbilical cord-derived mesenchymal stem cells) to treat the lung damage of the most severe cases of COVID-19. Although designed to test for safety, the trial showed the treatment repaired the lungs and also halted the disease.

It is with great humility that I acknowledge all those who made this clinical trial possible, 100 percent funded by generous donors. We are especially grateful to the Barilla Group and Barilla Family, Ugo Colombo, the Fondazione Tronchetti Provera, the Simkins Family Foundation, and the many friends and family in Italy, who allowed us to get started without delay in our cell manufacturing, regulatory process and early clinical trial.

We are also incredibly thankful to NABTU (North America's Building Trade Unions) whose major grant allowed us to complete the initial clinical trial and to quickly begin manufacturing cell products for expanded clinical trials and expanded use protocols. We can now establish a repository of therapeutic cell products to distribute UC-MSC doses to centers and hospitals in North America for rapid response and intervention,

With new funds and awareness raised by publication of this book, and the continuing generosity of our donors, The Cure Alliance will continue to support collaborative efforts to prevent and cure COVID-19 and future pandemics in the U.S. and around the world

With this success, we stand on the shoulders of the DRIF (Diabetes Research Institute Foundation) which over decades funded the critically important building blocks of cell therapy research at the DRI (Diabetes Research Institute). The knowledge gained by the DRI clinical trials, specifically the role UC-MSCs might play in curing diabetes T-1, led scientists to seek trials for COVID-19.

Of course, none of the above would have ever come together if not for the integrity, knowledge, leadership and lifelong humanitarian efforts of Dr. Camillo Ricordi, the principal investigator of the UC-MSC trial, the Director of the DRI and founder of The Cure Alliance. For the past 10 years, I have personally watched how he works: he imagines medical miracles, then makes them happen, under the strictest scientific guidelines. At the start of the COVID-19 outbreak, he instantly assembled a team of over a dozen top scientific collaborators from China and across America. For the trial, he assembled a dedicated and tireless group of nurses and healthcare workers. He stayed at the hospital each day, in donated protective gear, overseeing the infusions, administering the intravenous himself when nurses were called away for more critical emergencies. Miami, where the clinical trial took place, had become a COVID-19 war zone. These unsung heroes are so much a part of the success.

Which brings us to a final, and most heartfelt expression of gratitude: to the patients and their families who agreed to participate in our randomized controlled study (RCT), the gold standard requested by the FDA. They all enrolled in this trial knowing there was a 50 percent chance of receiving the stem cell treatment, a 50 percent chance of receiving a placebo. We honor their courage and willingness to sacrifice in order to contribute to science and help end this devastating pandemic.

— Shelley Ross

A huge thank you to Door No. 3 Design.

Creating this book has been a true labor of love, and this team of talented ladies worked with me every step of the way. They made my ideas come alive in every spread of this book.

And thanks to Hank (for being Hank) – the DN3 coffee-drinking, beer-loving pooch who doesn't always get it right...but never stops trying.

Kobalt

SUPPORTS

THE
CURE
ALLIANCE

DSW ENTERTAINMENT

SUPPORTS

LOVE FOUNDATION
Founded by Michael E. Love

SUPPORTS

Don't Stop Believin' • Something Just Like This • Shape Of You • Girls Like You • Don't Let Me Down
• Castle On The Hill • Sweet Dreams (Are Made Of This) • What About Us • Love Yourself
In My Blood • Closer • No Tears Left To Cry • High Hopes • Look What You Made Me Do
• There's Nothing Holdin' Me Back • Beautiful Trauma • What Lovers Do • Treat You Better
Uptown Funk • Photograph • Havana • Happier • Separate Ways/Worlds Apart • Faithfully
• Breathin • Livin' On A Prayer • Wanted Dead Or Alive • Single Ladies (Put A Ring On It)
Anyway You Want It • God Is A Woman • River • Locked Out Of Heaven • Roses • Shallow • Sick Boy
• Love Me Again • Supermarket   New Man • Trumpets • Back To
Flowers • Paris • Break Up With   Black • Know No Better • Rise
Your Girlfriend, I'm Bored •   2U • What Do You Mean?
Smooth • Set Fire To The Rain •   Mama • Marry You • Nothing
• Skin • Umbrella • Close To Me   Breaks Like A Heart • So Far
GreenLight • GalwayGirl • Feels   Away • Don't Wanna Know
• Rockabye • I Don't Wanna Live   • Lost In Japan • Hey Loo
Forever • #Selfie • We Are Young   Ma, I Made It • All We Know
• Stone In Love • All Time Low •   Wait • Live In The Moment
These Days • Best Of Me • It's My Life   • Here Comes The Rain Again
• You Give Love A Bad Name •   Let's Stay Together • Treasure
Baby • Just The Way You Are   • Wheel In The Sky • Heart
• Handclap • Great Are You   Don't Break Around Her
Lord When • I Was Your Man •   • Despacito (Remix) • Stitches
Eraser • Dive • Cold Water   We Are Family • Hurt Somebody
• 2002 • Symphony • Moves Like   • Naked • Needed Me
Jagger • Issues • Open Arms •   Blame • Love My Life • Brave
• Believe • Titanium • Story Of My Life • Now Or Never • Call It What You Want • Who's Crying Now
There Must Be An Angel (Playing With My Heart) • I'm The One • Nancy Mulligan • Some Night
• Everybody Hates Me • Tenerife Sea • What Do I Know? • Too Much To Ask • Bloodstream
Drag Me Down • Only The Young • 1-800-273-8255 • Lights • Stand By You • Rearview Town
• Runaway Baby • Scared To Be Lonely • All The Small Things • Electricity • Come And Get It
I Predict A Riot • Disturbia • Not Giving In • Mercy • Getaway Car • Bed • Grenade • All Of The Star
• Payphone • Yeah • The Lazy Song • Don't Let Go (Love) • Barcelona • Honest • Me, Myself & I
It Will Rain • Blue Jeans • Maps • They Don't Know • Would I Lie To You? • Flatliner • New Year's Do
• Perfect • Places Sisters Are Doin' It For Themselves • XO • With You • Good Times

HIPGNOSIS SONGS FUND